10 MINUTE
MOMENTS
SERIES

BR

SEEKING JUSTICE

EXPLORING GOD'S
PERSPECTIVE
TEN MINUTES
AT A TIME

 simply for students

YouthMinistry.com/TOGETHER

10 Minute Moments: Seeking Justice
Exploring God's Perspective Ten Minutes at a Time

© 2013 Brian Cress

group.com
simplyyouthministry.com

All rights reserved. No part of this book may be reproduced in any manner whatsoever without prior written permission from the publisher, except where noted in the text and in the case of brief quotations embodied in critical articles and reviews. For information, visit group.com/customer-support/permissions.

Credits
Author: Brian Cress
Executive Developer: Jason Ostrander
Chief Creative Officer: Joani Schultz
Editor: Rob Cunningham
Cover Art and Production: Veronica Preston

Unless otherwise indicated, all Scripture quotations are taken from the Holy Bible, New Living Translation, copyright © 1996, 2004, 2007 by Tyndale House Foundation. Used by permission of Tyndale House Publishers, Inc., Carol Stream, Illinois 60188. All rights reserved.

Scripture quotations marked (NIV) are taken from the Holy Bible, New International Version®, NIV®. Copyright © 1973, 1978, 1984, 2011 by Biblica, Inc.™ Used by permission of Zondervan. All rights reserved worldwide. www.zondervan.com The "NIV" and "New International Version" are trademarks registered in the United States Patent and Trademark Office by Biblica, Inc.™

ISBN 978-1-4707-1029-3

10 9 8 7 6 5 4 3   20 19 18 17 16 15 14

Printed in the U.S.A.

CONTENTS

INTRODUCTION

Kumar is a young guy who's probably not too different from you. He works his hardest at school and is learning new skills in his after-school internship. He likes sports and keeps up with new music. He's always joking around with his friends. If you met him, like I did, I bet you'd have a lot to talk about.

But there's something about Kumar's past that's hard to believe: When he was just a kid, Kumar was held as a slave. That's right—a slave. He had to make bricks all day, every day. He wasn't free to leave the brick factory. The owner beat him up.

I bet it makes you mad to know that a guy like Kumar was held as a slave. And I bet it makes you even madder to know that he's not the only one—experts tell us that there are millions of slaves in the world today.

When I first heard these numbers as a youth pastor, it floored me. I wanted to jump in with both feet and do something about it. Chances are you want to do something, too.

What I discovered along the way was that God does not like this injustice either. In fact, all throughout the Bible, I began to find verse after verse about God's passion for justice. Once I had a passion for justice, these verses jumped off the page at me—but somehow, even though I'd been reading my Bible for years, I'd missed them before.

This devotional is all about helping you encounter some of those Scriptures that have been so important on this justice journey—along with stories of real people who have experienced injustice and stories of students just like you from across the globe who are doing something about it. To help protect individuals' privacy, I've changed the names of some people you'll read about in this devotional, but all the stories are true.

These days I have the privilege of working with a global team of Christian lawyers, social workers, investigators, and community activists who are trying to answer God's call to do justice. We are called International Justice Mission. We come alongside local governments and partners throughout the developing world to rescue victims of violence (such as slavery and sex trafficking) and to bring criminals to justice under local laws. We restore survivors to safety and strength (helping them find jobs, providing long-term trauma therapy and counseling, and more), and we help local law enforcement build a safe future that lasts—so that vulnerable people aren't abused and enslaved in the first place.

But as you'll see from the stories in this devotional, you don't have to be a lawyer, investigator, or social worker like my co-workers to make a difference. You don't even have to be an adult. As you read these verses and stories, listen to what God is nudging you to do, because you can make a difference today.

Seek Justice,

Brian Cress
Director of Student Mobilization—Youth
International Justice Mission (ijm.org)

DAY ZERO

Every great idea, accomplishment, event, habit, or life-change has a "Day Zero." It's that day you decide to start something new. It's that day you decide to try out for a sport. It's that day you decide to start saving money for a car. It's that day you decide to learn how to play an instrument. It's that day you start studying hard to pass a big final exam.

I remember my "Day Zero" when I decided to start running a couple of years ago. I had just come home from a doctor's appointment, and the scale in his office showed my weight was way more than I wanted. I decided right then that I wanted to lose some weight, and I set a goal to run a half marathon. It was my "Day Zero." So my plan included things such as finding the time to run, getting the right shoes to wear, planning out how many days a week I would run and how long my runs would be, and other important details.

I started off slow, by walking a mile several days a week. That grew to jogging a mile several days a week, then two miles, and so on, until I was able to run a half marathon—and lost the weight I wanted. It did not happen overnight; in fact, it took six months. But one thing happened along the way: Running became something that I looked forward to on almost a daily basis. It became a part of my life. Now I have completed three half marathons, lost 40 pounds, subscribe to running magazines, and even raised thousands of dollars for International Justice Mission by running, and it all started because I had a "Day Zero" when I started making a plan.

The same is true with reading the Bible. Coming up with your plan will help you succeed. So today is your "Day Zero," the day to make your plan. This is the beginning of a journey to discover what the Bible has to say about God's passion for justice.

HERE'S HOW TO GET STARTED:

1. PICK THE DAYS

Set a goal of how many days each week you are going to read, and circle the ones you'll start with below. Increase the number of reading days as you go from week to week. Remember, just like my running, it's fine to start slow and build. Don't be discouraged along the way if you miss a day or two; that happens to us all. What matters is that you pick it back up.

This devotional has 31 days. Maybe reading the Bible is already a daily part of your life, or maybe you're feeling really motivated to make a change. If that's you, you might want to do the 31 days straight in a row, learning something new about God's justice every day for a month.

Weeks 1 & 2 Goal: _____
Monday Tuesday Wednesday Thursday Friday Saturday Sunday

Weeks 3 & 4 Goal: _____
Monday Tuesday Wednesday Thursday Friday Saturday Sunday

Weeks 5 & 6 Goal: _____
Monday Tuesday Wednesday Thursday Friday Saturday Sunday

Weeks 7 & 8 Goal: _____
Monday Tuesday Wednesday Thursday Friday Saturday Sunday

2. PICK A TIME OF DAY
This will help you create consistency. The more specific you can be, the better.

_____ a.m. or _____ p.m.

3. PICK A PLACE
I recommend someplace that is not filled with distractions—maybe on the floor in your room, a comfortable chair in your living room, the kitchen counter, or even a local coffee shop. I would suggest that you pick someplace other than your bed, when you're about to fall asleep.

Place: _____

4. BRING YOUR BIBLE WITH YOU
Bring along a highlighter and a pen, too. You'll want to be able to quickly jot down your thoughts and reflections in this devotional, and each day you'll underline or highlight the key Scripture in your Bible as well, so you can easily return to it in the future. You may even want to write the date you studied the verse next to it in your Bible—in years to come, this will remind you of what God showed you during this time. Reading the Bible online, on your smartphone, or on a tablet is fine, too, but just a bit trickier for keeping your notes.

5. TELL SOMEONE YOUR GOAL
Having others who know about your goal to encourage you along the way is essential. I never would have made my goal of running a half marathon if I had not told anyone else

about it. Knowing that my wife, Lori, would ask me how my run went was often all the motivation I needed to put on my shoes and head out the door on those days when I simply did not want to run. It's especially helpful if the friend you tell about your goal has a similar goal to read the Bible and this devotional, too—you may even be in a small group that could do this study together.

Name of friend: _____

Now send this friend a text, email, or social media post telling them of your goal.

6. DAILY ACTION ITEMS

Each day you will be challenged to do something. Some of the ideas are ways to seek justice. Some of the ideas are ways to help what you've read sink in. The ideas listed are simply suggestions for you. If you sense God telling you to do something else, then go for it.

7. NOW PRAY AND ASK GOD TO

- give you success in reaching your reading plan goals

- give you fresh insights as you read each day

- give you ideas and actions you can take along the way

- make your heart and passion for justice to be in line with God's

WITH YOUR PLAN IN PLACE, WRITE YOUR DAY 1 DATE HERE: _____

Have you ever been standing in the "10 items or less" checkout line at the grocery store with your soda, chips, and candy bar, and you look at the basket of the person in front of you and they have 13 items? Feels like an injustice, right? Well, today in our society, the words *injustice* and *justice* can almost mean anything. So here are the definitions we will be using for this devotional book.

- Injustice is when someone abuses power to take from others the good things that God has given them— their life, liberty, and the fruits of their love and labor.

- Justice is about using power rightly—to make sure everyone is safe, defended, and protected.

Justice comes up a lot in the Bible regarding how we treat people who have less power than we do—people who are vulnerable.

Often, when we think about what's just and unjust, we think of governments: judges sentencing criminals for their crimes, police catching bad guys. That's true—this is an important picture of justice, and it's one that we'll return to a few times in this study. But just because you're not a judge or police officer doesn't mean that you don't have a role to play in doing justice. You see, justice is about using power—and we all have power. God calls you to use the power you have to make sure that everyone—especially people who are weak or vulnerable—is treated fairly.

TODAY'S READING:

- Find today's verses, highlight them, and add today's date next to them in your own Bible.

- Read the verses several times, thinking about each word and asking God to help you understand what these Scriptures mean.

ECCLESIASTES 4:1

Again, I observed all the oppression that takes place under the sun. I saw the tears of the oppressed, with no one to comfort them. The oppressors have great power, and their victims are helpless.

2 CORINTHIANS 5:20

So we are Christ's ambassadors; God is making his appeal through us.

QUESTIONS TO THINK ABOUT:

- What are some ways you see power being abused in our world today? What are some specific local examples that come to mind?

- What are some of the powers that you have? Circle all that apply: social, financial, intellectual, athletic, musical, other.

- What are some ways power can be used for good? for evil?

- Why do you think God chooses to use us as his ambassadors?

DAILY ACTION ITEM:
- What is one of the powers you have that you can use for good today?

PRAY:
Before you move on to what's next in your day, pause a few moments and pray for any work of justice God might be asking you to begin at your school.

THOUGHTS:
This space is for any notes or thoughts you would like to write down.

In sports, percentages are typically used as a way to measure an athlete's skill. For example, in baseball, if you actually hit the ball and make it to base one out of every three times you're up to bat, you are hitting .333, which is fantastic. But in basketball, someone making one out of three free throws is considered a bad free-throw shooter. When playing golf on a "par three" hole, getting the ball in the hole in three hits is considered average—but most of us take four or five tries! In tennis, you only get two tries to serve the ball into the correct spot, and then if you miss, the other player gets a point.

To be considered excellent in any sport, you must follow the advice of coaches and get lots of practice to move your percentage to the highest level. This idea is actually in the Bible, too. Did you know that one of the prophets in the Bible talks about going three for three? Read on to see how.

TODAY'S READING:

- Find today's verse, highlight it, and add today's date next to it in your own Bible.

- Read the verse several times, thinking about each word and asking God to help you understand what it means.

MICAH 6:8

O people, the Lord has told you what is good, and this is what he requires of you: to do what is right, to love mercy, and to walk humbly with your God.

QUESTIONS TO THINK ABOUT:

- Why do you think God sees these things as required actions rather than just suggestions?

- In your own words, write a brief definition or explanation of these three phrases.

    1. To do what is right / to seek justice =
    _____

    2. To love mercy =
    _____

    3. To walk humbly with your God =
    _____

- Now list specific ways that you, your youth group, or your school can do these things.

    1. To do what is right / to seek justice =
    _____

    2. To love mercy =
    _____

    3. To walk humbly with your God =
    _____

It's OK if you can't think of something for each area. For many of us, justice is the one thing we have the hardest time figuring out how to actually do. As you journey through this devotional, you will find all sorts of ways that you will be able to add seeking justice to your daily life. Remember, doing these things is not what makes you a Christian, but simply is the way you live out your faith.

DAILY ACTION ITEM:

- Text, email, or call the friend you chose to share this justice journey with on your "Day Zero" planning. If you didn't pick a friend to share with, then post on social media about your thoughts today.

PRAY:

Before you move on to what's next in your day, pray and ask God to give you a clear picture over the coming weeks of what seeking justice can look like in your life.

THOUGHTS:

This space is for any notes or thoughts you would like to write down.

As a senior, Summer (her name, not the season) was involved in her school's production of the musical *Beauty and the Beast*, playing the role of Belle. Along with pouring her life into the musical, she wanted to find a way to merge her passion for music with her passion for justice. The musical brought large numbers of people through the doors of her high school, so this was a crucial opportunity to draw people's attention to a world of suffering that is often ignored—and to the ways that others could help.

Summer discovered a local costume shop that sold artificial light-up roses as fundraisers for musicals, and she knew she'd hit gold. The school's Justice Club bought hundreds of them and sold them at every showing of the musical to raise money to help victims of injustice.

At the end of every performance, when the entire cast filled the stage, everyone lifted their roses high in the air, holding out the message that light persists even in the darkest places.

Who knew that singing in a high school musical could be one way to sing about God's justice?

- Find today's verse, highlight it, and add today's date next to it in your own Bible.

- Read the verse several times, thinking about each word and asking God to help you understand what it means.

PSALM 101:1

I will sing of your love and justice, Lord. I will praise you with songs.

QUESTIONS TO THINK ABOUT:

- How important is music in your life? What are some specific ways you see that importance demonstrated?

- Can you think of three songs about love? Easy, right? What about songs about justice?

    1.

    2.

    3.

- Why don't we often think of singing songs about God's justice?

- Why would God want us to use music as a way of expressing justice? What are some specific ways you can do this?

DAILY ACTION ITEM:

- Search for a song about justice you could purchase and download. (Stumped? You may want to check out these songs: "I Saw What I Saw" by Sara Groves, "Do Something" by Matthew West, and "Set My People Free" by Dara Maclean.)

- Sit down at the piano, pick up your guitar, or write some lyrics that God might be putting in your head.

PRAY:

Before you move on to what's next in your day, pray and ask God to help you seek justice in and through your music.

THOUGHTS:

This space is for any notes or thoughts you would like to write down.

During my ninth-grade art class, a guy named Dennis seemed to always get picked on by the "cool crowd." You see, Dennis had some physical and mental disabilities that made him an easy target to blame for spilled paint and dirty paintbrushes, and he was always the last person chosen for any group art projects. I must admit it was easy for me to sit back and never speak up for him or go against the crowd. I'll never forget the day my friend Scott convinced me to join him in standing up against the crowd for Dennis. We invited him to join our table and be a part of our art project team. We made it known to the rest of the crowd that Dennis was "off limits" for any more wrong accusations, criticism, or simply being made fun of. I remember Dennis becoming a special friend to many of us during the rest of that school year. Sometimes justice means standing up for others—especially for people who are vulnerable or who don't have a lot of power of their own.

TODAY'S READING:

- Find today's verse, highlight it, and add today's date next to it in your own Bible.

- Read the verse several times, thinking about each word and asking God to help you understand what it means.

EXODUS 23:2

"You must not follow the crowd in doing wrong. When you are called to testify in a dispute, do not be swayed by the crowd to twist justice."

QUESTIONS TO THINK ABOUT:

- Why is it so easy to follow the crowd in doing wrong?

- When have you made the tough choice to go against the crowd and do the right thing? What was that experience like?

- When has another person stood up for you? What did you learn from that?

- In which area of your life is it most difficult to stand against the crowd? Why?

DAILY ACTION ITEM:

- Can you think of someone at your school that the "crowd" picks on? What's one specific thing you and your friends can do this week to stand up for that person?

    1. Sit with this person at lunch

    2. Invite him or her to join your study group

    3. Other ideas: _____

PRAY:

Before you move on to what's next in your day, pause a few moments and pray for the courage to stand up against the crowd that you sometimes face.

THOUGHTS:

This space is for any notes or thoughts you would like to write down.

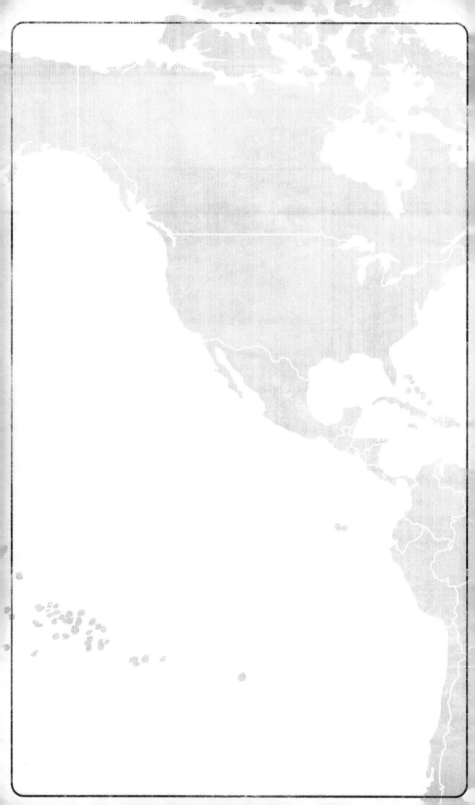

DAY 5

_____

"What am I going to wear today?" Is this a daily dilemma for you? You might try on several items before settling on an outfit, and even then you might change one more time. Or maybe you're more like me. I'm a "whatever shirt happens to be next on the closet hanger" kind of guy. However, one of my favorite T-shirts is from a trip to Kolkata, India, that I took with my son Graydon. He actually picked out the shirt for me: It's black and has the signatures—in white Hindi script down the side—of 20 young women who make these shirts at an organization called Freeset.

These girls and women used to be abused every day by men who would pay to exploit their bodies. But now, instead of being forced to work as prostitutes, these brave women are free and can make a living they are proud of by producing these cool T-shirts and handbags. That's what Freeset is all about: providing a new opportunity and a good job for these women.

The best thing about this shirt is that complete strangers standing in line at stores will ask me what the shirt means. It then gives me a chance to share about my passion for justice.

- Find today's verse, highlight it, and add today's date next to it in your own Bible.

- Read the verse several times, thinking about each word and asking God to help you understand what it means.

JOB 29:14

"Everything I did was honest. Righteousness covered me like a robe, and I wore justice like a turban."

QUESTIONS TO THINK ABOUT:

- How are honesty, righteousness, and justice linked together?

- Can you have one of these characteristics without the others? Why or why not?

- Think about the phrase "everything I did" from today's Scripture. What might be something you can do at school today to show righteousness—in other words, a right way of living that honors God?

- Think about the clothes in your closet—or go stand in front of your clothes as you consider this question. What messages might your clothes or hats tell others about the type of person you are?

DAILY ACTION ITEM:

- Do you have some clothes in your closet that no longer fit and would be great to give to someone else? Grab a bag and fill it up with clothes you could give to a local organization that works with children and families in your community.

- Take Slavery Footprint's online quiz to see how many slaves might be making the products—including clothes—that you use every day: slaveryfootprint.org.

PRAY:

Before you move on to what's next in your day, pause a few moments and pray for the girls and women still trapped in sex trafficking and for justice to come for them.

THOUGHTS:

This space is for any notes or thoughts you would like to write down.

Have you ever been really thirsty? I mean get-sick-because-you-are-seriously-dehydrated thirsty? I remember going hiking with some college friends out near Palm Springs, California. My first mistake was not bringing along a water bottle, but since we were hiking along a stream, I figured I would be OK. My second mistake was ignoring the weatherman saying it was a beautiful, sunny 105 degrees when we started out. Then the third and biggest mistake was following the advice of my friend to take a "shortcut" over a ridge to get to our final destination: a waterfall into a natural swimming pool in the rocks. Needless to say, several hours later—experiencing dehydration sickness, sunburns, and sunstroke—I ran with all my remaining energy, speed, and strength to the water's edge and, falling in face first, drank until I could drink no more.

Have you ever heard about being "thirsty" for justice? Read on.

TODAY'S READING:

- Find today's verse, highlight it, and add today's date next to it in your own Bible.

- Read the verse several times, thinking about each word and asking God to help you understand what it means.

MATTHEW 5:6

"God blesses those who hunger and thirst for justice, for they will be satisfied."

QUESTIONS TO THINK ABOUT:

- Why is it significant that this verse uses the words *hunger* and *thirst*?

- How do you think God blesses people who do justice?

- Think of a time you did something that really satisfied you. What made it so satisfying?

- What are some ways you could begin to hunger and thirst for justice—or hunger and thirst for it even more than you already do?

DAILY ACTION ITEM:

- Intentionally skip making a lunch or taking lunch money to school today so that you actually can experience hunger. When people ask why you are not eating, tell them about your hunger for justice to be done for those trapped in slavery.

- Make a sack lunch that you could give to someone who is asking for money at an intersection or the freeway on-ramp near your home or school.

PRAY:

Before you move on to what's next in your day, pause a few moments and pray for people in your community who may be hungry.

THOUGHTS:

This space is for any notes or thoughts you would like to write down.

DAY 7

What comes to mind when you see the word *rock*? Maybe a type of music? Something you like to climb on? Thirteen-year-old Viswanathan was forced to think about rocks all day long. He spent time inside a rock quarry (a place where large rocks are broken into smaller rocks) in India for eight years. His family was held in slavery. His parents worked 13 to 16 hours a day, using sledgehammers to break huge boulders into rocks that could be used for roads and sidewalks. As a teenager, Viswanathan used smaller hammers to crush rocks into gravel to be used for pathways and roads. His dreams of going to school and one day being a doctor or police officer could never become a reality.

But all of this changed one day when local government officials, supported by an anti-slavery team from International Justice Mission, did a rescue operation at this rock quarry and freed his family from the slavery of breaking rocks. Viswanathan was able to trade in his life of slavery for school—and the opportunity to pursue his dreams.

TODAY'S READING:

- Find today's verse, highlight it, and add today's date next to it in your own Bible.

- Read the verse several times, thinking about each word and asking God to help you understand what it means.

DEUTERONOMY 32:4

"He is the Rock; his deeds are perfect. Everything he does is just and fair. He is a faithful God who does no wrong; how just and upright he is!"

QUESTIONS TO THINK ABOUT:

- Why do you think God is referred to as "the Rock"? What characteristics of a rock are also true of God?

- How has God been a "rock" in your life?

- Is there a difference between something that is fair and something that is just? Explain your reasons.

- What are some ways that God's justice and fairness can be demonstrated today through your church or other organizations?

DAILY ACTION ITEM:

- Find a medium-size rock that you carry in your pocket all day today at school. Place it on your desk, lunch table, or dinner table at home. Use any opportunities you might have to tell others about the slaves in our world today when people ask you about the rock.

PRAY:

Before you move on to what's next in your day, pause a few moments and pray for the other teenagers like Viswanathan who are still slaves in rock quarries in South Asia and around the world.

THOUGHTS:

This space is for any notes or thoughts you would like to write down.

Robbie really wanted to make a difference at his high school by raising awareness about modern-day slavery and sex trafficking. First he tried to get approval to speak in a class or assembly. He waited and waited, only to be told no. Then he tried to get it included in one of his school's fundraising projects, and he waited and waited, only to be told no again. Then he traveled to the state capital to meet with state representatives about these issues, and he waited and waited, only to be told no again.

Robbie then asked to give a presentation at church, and he waited and waited, and finally got a yes! Next he planned a pizza party for his peers to share about justice, and his peers said yes. Then he asked to meet with a member of Congress, and he waited again—but got another yes! Robbie is now in university pursuing a degree in political science. Robbie recently told me, "My passion for justice has deepened my heart for God. I simply want to use the gifts and skills God gave me to make a difference for others." The waiting paid off!

TODAY'S READING:

- Find today's passage, highlight it, and add today's date next to it in your own Bible.

- Read the passage several times, thinking about each word and asking God to help you understand what it means.

JOB 35:13-14

"But it is wrong to say God doesn't listen, to say the Almighty isn't concerned. You say you can't see him, but he will bring justice if you will only wait."

QUESTIONS TO THINK ABOUT:

- Is it really wrong to say, "God doesn't listen"? Why or why not? (Consider reading the whole chapter of today's passage from Job; you will get a feel for what is going on with this story.)

- What are some things you have been calling out to God and waiting for?

- Why do you think God waits to take action?

- What action might God be waiting for you to take?

DAILY ACTION ITEM:

- Make-up day! Pick one action item from the previous days that you haven't done—something God might be waiting for you to do today. Or if you've done them all, choose your favorite and do it again!

PRAY:

Before you move on to what's next in your day, pause a few moments and pray for the other students like Robbie who are waiting for ways to share about ending slavery.

THOUGHTS:

This space is for any notes or thoughts you would like to write down.

Have you heard or sung the song "The Heart of Worship" by Matt Redman? Pause for a moment and go listen to the song, if you have a copy of it. Or look up the lyrics online and read them.

Back in the late 1990s Matt's Redman's home church in England was struggling to find the real meaning and purpose behind their worship on Sunday mornings. So the church did a pretty remarkable thing: They got rid of the sound system and band and decided to gather together with just their voices. They apparently had some times of awkward silence, a cappella singing, and prayers from the heart, but they were encountering God in a fresh, new way that did not require anything more than an open heart and simple voices to praise God.

They eventually did bring back the sound system and musicians. Redman wrote the song "The Heart of Worship" about the experience. Yet the idea of empty worship did not originate with Redman's church, as we see in today's Scripture.

TODAY'S READING:

- Find today's passage, highlight it, and add today's date next to it in your own Bible.

- Read the passage several times, thinking about each word and asking God to help you understand what it means.

AMOS 5:23-24

"Away with your noisy hymns of praise! I will not listen to the music of your harps. Instead, I want to see a mighty flood of justice, an endless river of righteous living."

QUESTIONS TO THINK ABOUT:

- Why is it so much easier to simply sing or talk about issues than to actually do something?

- Why is God not pleased with our worship if our lives aren't filled with justice and right living?

- Picture a flood of water covering over land—how might that image help you relate to a "flood of justice" compared to simply a "creek" or "stream" of justice?

- Justice and righteous living go hand in hand together. Write down the names of several people who are good examples of justice and righteous living. What can you learn from them?

DAILY ACTION ITEM:

- Call, text, post, email, or write to one of the people you listed in that last question. Thank that person for being such a solid example of justice and right living.

PRAY:

Before you move on to what's next in your day, pause a few moments and pray for a flood of students to rise up and do something for justice.

THOUGHTS:

This space is for any notes or thoughts you would like to write down.

I remember a time I got angry—I mean, really angry. It was when I first heard about modern-day slavery. My own daughter Brittany was 12 years old when I heard a story about a girl her age being trafficked. As I listened to the story, it felt like my own daughter was the one who was kidnapped.

I'm going to tell you a story about a girl named Alisha, and I bet it will make you angry, too. Try to imagine how you'd feel if Alisha were someone you knew personally—a friend, a classmate, a sister.

Alisha was only 12 years old when she was taken from Nepal to India—trafficked across borders—and sold to a brothel, a place where people go to engage in sexual activity. Overnight, this became Alisha's world: a brothel in the middle of Kolkata's notorious red-light district. The brothel madam told Alisha that she would have to work like the other girls for her food and her rent. If she refused to service a customer, she would not get any food. Alone in a foreign city, Alisha had nowhere else to go. For five years, she was trapped inside the dark nightmare.

But then one day, everything changed. IJM had been gathering evidence in that very brothel, and acting on this evidence, the police rescued Alisha and 16 other girls who had been trafficked. In aftercare, Alisha slowly started to open up, and shared that she was pregnant. Today she and her child have settled into a long-term aftercare home where she is a vibrant and dedicated mother.

The Bible shows that God gets angry when he sees oppression and injustice. When we hear stories of injustice like Alisha's, we may get angry, too. We need to ask God to direct that anger to action.

TODAY'S READING:

- Find today's verse, highlight it, and add today's date next to it in your own Bible.

- Read the verse several times, thinking about each word and asking God to help you understand what it means.

PSALM 7:6

Arise, O Lord, in anger! Stand up against the fury of my enemies! Wake up, my God, and bring justice!

QUESTIONS TO THINK ABOUT:

- What might be the difference between good anger and bad anger?

- Do you think God was asleep and had to be awakened? If not, then what was the psalmist communicating in this verse?

- What are three things that really make you angry? Why do they stir anger inside of you?

- How might you channel your anger into standing up for justice? Think of specific ways.

DAILY ACTION ITEM:

- Take a red marker and mark a large X on the back of your hand to represent your desire to end slavery. Share your anger with anyone who asks what it means.

PRAY:

Before you move on to what's next in your day, pause a few moments and pray for people still trapped in slavery.

THOUGHTS:

This space is for any notes or thoughts you would like to write down.

DATE:

Sandana was only 12 years old, but her voice was the one that would make all the difference. She and her parents, along with other families gathered together, had just been rescued from forced labor slavery at a rice mill, where rice is dried, bagged, and shipped to markets. It was a terrible place: The owners of the rice mill refused to let the workers leave, they beat them, and they even doused one slave's arm in kerosene and set it on fire as punishment.

But now that the families stood before a government official with the authority to free them from slavery, they were too afraid to tell the truth—the owners had twisted the truth and threatened to kill them if they ever told anyone what was happening in the rice mill.

One by one, the defeated slaves followed the way of the crowd and denied that they were being forced to work or were being abused. That is, until Sandana stepped forward. Though she was young, she found the courage to do what the slave owners feared the most: She spoke the truth. Sandana explained that her dad couldn't tell the truth, that the owner beat her father, and that everybody else was too afraid to say what was really happening.

Struck by the raw power of innocent truth and her courage in speaking out, the government official set all of the families free and gave them official release certificates out of a life of slavery.

45

- Find today's verse, highlight it, and add today's date next to it in your own Bible.

- Read the verse several times, thinking about each word and asking God to help you understand what it means.

PSALM 40:9

I have told all your people about your justice. I have not been afraid to speak out, as you, O Lord, well know.

QUESTIONS TO THINK ABOUT:

- What can make you afraid to speak out about something you see that is wrong?

- What might be some ways to overcome these fears?

- When have you seen another person courageously stand up for what is right—or when have you done that? What did you learn from that experience?

- Today's verse is actually a prayer or song being shared to God. How might prayer help you speak out?

DAILY ACTION ITEM:

- Write out a prayer or song to God about some of the fears you are facing or trying to stand up for.

PRAY:

Before you move on to what's next in your day, pause a few moments and pray for other young people like Sandana.

THOUGHTS:

This space is for any notes or thoughts you would like to write down.

Kathy never really considered herself an athlete. She had a bike, but she didn't ride it often.

But her senior year in high school, Kathy learned about an opportunity to go on a five-day, 550-mile bike ride from one symbol of the fight against slavery—the National Underground Railroad Museum in Cincinnati, Ohio—all the way to another—the Lincoln Memorial in Washington, D.C. The ride would raise awareness and funds to fight modern-day slavery.

Darcy, on the other hand, is an athlete. As a volleyball player, she strives to stay in top physical condition, which includes doing pushups—lots of pushups. After hearing about other girls her age who were trapped in slavery, she decided to raise awareness and funds by doing…push-ups. And would you believe she did 1,866 push-ups?!?

Both girls decided to make a difference by doing something that would bring a voice to the voiceless. They simply chose to use the muscles in their arms and legs to do the talking. Oh, and between these two girls, they raised $5,875.38 to help rescue others!

- Find today's passage, highlight it, and add today's date next to it in your own Bible.

- Read the passage several times, thinking about each word and asking God to help you understand what it means.

PROVERBS 31:8-9

Speak up for those who cannot speak for themselves; ensure justice for those being crushed. Yes, speak up for the poor and helpless, and see that they get justice.

QUESTIONS TO THINK ABOUT:

- How are the poor and helpless the victims of injustice in our world today?

- How is justice ensured in our country today?

- What people at your school or church have stood up for victims of injustice?

- List some of the skills and gifts that you have that might be used to "speak up" (such as art, sports, writing, music, drama, and so on).

DAILY ACTION ITEM:

- Do an online search for an organization or church in your community hosting an event where you could participate or use your gifts to serve this month.

PRAY:

Before you move on to what's next in your day, pause a few moments and pray for an opportunity to speak up for those who cannot speak for themselves.

THOUGHTS:

This space is for any notes or thoughts you would like to write down.

DATE:
_____

Kumar was an orphan. He was poor. No one was looking out for him.

This kid with no defenders was an easy target for a corrupt business owner, who offered a job to Kumar—an offer that turned out to just be a trick to trap Kumar as a slave in his brick factory.

Kumar struggled alongside adults at the brick kiln, bewildered and scared by what he saw. All day, every day, seven days a week, he carried heavy clay bricks back and forth in the brick kiln as they dried. Every moment was occupied. He worked seven days every week, never getting a day off or a vacation. He woke early each morning to begin laboring at 6:30 a.m. and continued until the evening hours, his hands raw and his body exhausted from the strain of making bricks all day long.

My co-workers in South Asia discovered what was happening to Kumar, and brought a report to local law enforcement. They partnered with local government authorities and police, who did a rescue operation at the factory to release the slaves. Kumar was brought to freedom after three years of forced labor. No longer a slave, Kumar had the opportunity to succeed in school—and to serve as an intern with IJM! As an intern, he gets to be a part of the team that once rescued him.

- Find today's verse, highlight it, and add today's date next to it in your own Bible.

- Read the verse several times, thinking about each word and asking God to help you understand what it means.

ISAIAH 1:17

"Learn to do good. Seek justice. Help the oppressed. Defend the cause of orphans. Fight for the rights of widows."

QUESTIONS TO THINK ABOUT:

- Circle each of the action words in today's verse. What would the opposite action look like?

- When thinking about the cause of justice, what is the power of each action word in this verse?

- Underline the words the actions are attached to. What would the opposite of those actions look like?

- Now write out what a Christian "job description" might sound like using all these items.

DAILY ACTION ITEM:

- Put a bandage around your index finger to remind yourself to do at least one good thing for someone else today. We discover issues of injustice by taking the time to notice what's going on around us. Maybe your act of goodness will be the help someone needs today.

PRAY:

Before you move on to what's next in your day, pause a few moments and pray for God to show you one good thing to do.

THOUGHTS:

This space is for any notes or thoughts you would like to write down.

During the 2013 Super Bowl—the game is the largest televised event in the United States each year—something strange happened just after the start of the third quarter. The lights went out! For the next 34 minutes, no one knew what to do. Some spectators began to scramble for the exits, players on the field didn't know what to do, and all of us watching on TV wondered if something bad was about to happen. Well, it turned out to be simply some overloaded electrical circuits.

Have you had the power go out at your house when doing homework or watching TV? It's a hassle, isn't it? Not much gets done—we depend on light, especially when it's dark outside. In Jesus' time, light was a game changer, too, and he speaks to this in today's Scripture.

TODAY'S READING:

- Find today's passage, highlight it, and add today's date next to it in your own Bible.

- Read the passage several times, thinking about each word and asking God to help you understand what it means.

MATTHEW 5:14-16 (NIV)

"You are the light of the world. A town built on a hill cannot be hidden. Neither do people light a lamp and put it under a bowl. Instead they put it on its stand, and it gives light to everyone in the house. In the same way, let your light shine before others, that they may see your good deeds and glorify your Father in heaven."

QUESTIONS TO THINK ABOUT:

- Why is it significant that the first sentence of this passage is a statement rather than a question?

- Why is it meaningful that Jesus used two examples of light: one far away (city on a hill) and one close (room in a house)?

- Why does Jesus want others to see your good deeds?

- What are some ways you can be "light" in "dark" situations?

- Write down the names of two people in your life who are good examples of light.

DAILY ACTION ITEM:

- Have a "lights off" night at your house (or your next youth group meeting). No lights, TV, candles, or any other sources of light. Then allow yourself just five minutes with the lights on. What were those five minutes like? How did you feel about the light? Share your experience with others the next day on social media.

PRAY:

Before you move on to what's next in your day, pause a few moments and pray for ways you can be light today at your school or in your home.

THOUGHTS:

This space is for any notes or thoughts you would like to write down.

How many of you and your friends do you think you could cram into an old Volkswagen® Bug? Ten? Fifteen? Would you believe 20? That's the world record, and it was set by a group of students in Florida at the annual "Bug Jam"—a contest to fit as many people as possible in one of these little cars. The rules are simple: Each person must be at least 5 feet tall and 18 or older, and you need to be able to shut the doors and windows and keep them closed for five seconds.

But the students who pulled off this crazy stunt did it for more than getting into the *Guinness World Records*. They wanted to raise awareness and funds to fight human trafficking. Sometimes doing things a little out of the ordinary is what it takes to get the message out.

It's not just crazy college kids who do unexpected things to wake people up. In fact, the first message that Jesus gave at the start of his ministry was shocking to the people who heard it. Jesus stood up in the synagogue—the place where Jewish people meet to hear God's Word—and unrolled a scroll of Scripture. Then he read the verse that we'll focus on today. He didn't say anything beyond the reading—he just read it and then sat back down, leaving everyone to think. Let's just say that this got everyone's attention.

- Find today's passage, highlight it, and add today's date next to it in your own Bible.

- Read the passage several times, thinking about each word and asking God to help you understand what it means.

LUKE 4:18 (NIV)

"The Spirit of the Lord is on me, because he has anointed me to proclaim good news to the poor. He has sent me to proclaim freedom for the prisoners and recovery of sight for the blind, to set the oppressed free."

(In this passage, Jesus quotes from Isaiah 61—and if you have extra time today, read Luke 4:1-30 to get the whole picture of this Scripture)

QUESTIONS TO THINK ABOUT:

- Circle each of the things Jesus said he would do.

- How similar or different are each of these actions?

- Why do you think Jesus does more than just "proclaim" freedom?

- Who might be some of the "prisoners" or "oppressed" that need to be freed in our world today?

DAILY ACTION ITEM:

- Do something a bit crazy today to raise awareness for those oppressed. Here are some ideas:

    1. Make "chains" out of duct tape to wear all day at school.

    2. Style your hair in a crazy way that causes people to ask you what you are doing.

    3. Get creative with your own idea.

PRAY:

Before you move on to what's next in your day, pause a few moments and pray for people in our world who have yet to be freed from slavery.

THOUGHTS:

This space is for any notes or thoughts you would like to write down.

DATE:

_____

When Maadhav was a little boy, he started losing his vision. If he could have gone to a doctor, there's a chance something could have been done to help him. But Maadhav's family was enslaved—and that meant he couldn't get any medical attention.

By the time he was 12, he was virtually blind. But the rice mill owner didn't care. He made Maadhav work just like the others, because Maadhav was a slave. One time, the owner told Maadhav to turn on a machine that was used in the rice mill. He hesitated—new tasks were harder for him because he could not see. The owner beat him, demanding that Maadhav perform the job. When Maadhav started the machine, he got an electric shock. The owner would not let him go to the doctor.

Everything changed when IJM and local government authorities rescued Maadhav and seven families from two rice mills. At first, the government official did not believe that Maadhav could have worked as a slave because he was blind. But then Maadhav started acting out his duties, showing how he would rake the rice. He received justice that day and received the official certificate of release declaring him free from slavery. Maadhav's family settled into their lives of freedom, and Maadhav was able to start attending a special school for visually impaired students.

- Find today's verse, highlight it, and add today's date next to it in your own Bible.

- Read the verse several times, thinking about each word and asking God to help you understand what it means.

PSALM 82:3

"Give justice to the poor and the orphan; uphold the rights of the oppressed and the destitute."

QUESTIONS TO THINK ABOUT:

- Why are the poor and orphans so often treated unfairly?

- What rights do the poor often not receive?

- In what ways might the poor and orphans in your community be treated unfairly?

- List out two or three ideas that you, your school, or youth group could do to help the poor or orphans in your community.

DAILY ACTION ITEM:

- Find a box or grocery bag in your house and label it "Items for the food bank." Then ask your mom or dad which items your family can donate. Go around to a few neighbors and fill up the rest of the bag. Then deliver the bag sometime this week to a food bank in your community.

PRAY:

Before you move on to what's next in your day, pause a few moments and pray for the poor and oppressed in your community and around the world.

THOUGHTS:

This space is for any notes or thoughts you would like to write down.

I'll never forget my first trip to India. The sights, sounds, smells, and tastes were so different from what I was used to—like night is different from day. I remember sitting in a small stick shelter with a grass roof that was the temporary home to a family that had recently been rescued out of slavery. The mother in the family told me something incredible. Through a translator, she explained, "We have been pleading and crying out to God for years to be rescued, and the God of IJM sent you to rescue us." The social worker then turned and smiled at me and simply stated, "We have a good and just God, don't we?" My own praying took on a deeper meaning that day.

In today's verses you will see this same type of pleading happening in the prayers of David. In these psalms, David is reflecting on his feelings of fear and desperation for God's help, as he flees for his life from those who were oppressing him. (You can get the full story of why David was on the run in 1 Samuel 19.)

TODAY'S READING:

- Find today's verses, highlight them, and add today's date next to them in your own Bible.

- Read the verses several times, thinking about each word and asking God to help you understand what these Scriptures mean.

PSALM 17:1, 6-7

*O Lord, hear my plea for justice. Listen to my cry for help.
Pay attention to my prayer, for it comes from honest lips....I
am praying to you because I know you will answer, O God.
Bend down and listen as I pray. Show me your unfailing
love in wonderful ways. By your mighty power you rescue
those who seek refuge from their enemies.*

QUESTIONS TO THINK ABOUT:

- Circle the words in today's verses that are actions
  that the author is asking of God. Which of these items
  do you find most meaningful, and why?

- Why do you think the writer says the prayer "comes
  from honest lips"?

- Notice the psalmist's confidence that God would
  answer this prayer. Why do you think he was so
  confident in God?

- What can keep you from having that same
  confidence in God answering your prayers?

DAILY ACTION ITEM:

- Write out a prayer on the next page using many of
  the same action words that were used in today's
  verses.

PRAY:

Before you move on to what's next in your day, pause a few moments and pray the prayer you just wrote.

THOUGHTS

This space is for any notes or thoughts you would like to write down.

The students at the Trinity youth group in Kelowna, British Columbia, Canada, decided to get really serious about raising awareness and funds for rescuing slaves in our world. They formed a committee called "Freedom 151" to represent the 151 students in their middle school group and then set a goal of raising $151,000 over the next 12 months. Yes, you read that right: 151 middle school students set a goal to raise $151,000 in a year.

So how did they do something so huge? First they asked our huge God to help them, and then they got to work. They did bake sales, collected loose change, sold T-shirts, held a pancake breakfast, hosted a family pizza and fun night, organized concerts, and even had some guys do a snowboard-a-thon to raise money. What these students discovered along the way was that they did indeed have a huge God. It took a little longer than their 12-month goal, but in the end, they did raise the $151,000!

TODAY'S READING:

- Find today's verses, highlight them, and add today's date next to them in your own Bible.

- Read the verses several times, thinking about each word and asking God to help you understand what these Scriptures mean.

PSALM 36:5-6, 10

Your unfailing love, O Lord, is as vast as the heavens; your faithfulness reaches beyond the clouds. Your righteousness is like the mighty mountains, your justice like the ocean depths....Pour out your unfailing love on those who love you; give justice to those with honest hearts.

QUESTIONS TO THINK ABOUT:

- Circle the words that represent God's character. Now underline the words that describe those aspects of God's character.

- How and when have you seen these aspects of God's character in your life or in other people's lives?

- As with many psalms, parts of these verses are words to songs today. Why is it important for us to remember and acknowledge the hugeness of God?

- Very often God's justice is thought to be directed at those who are doing wrong, yet in these verses it is directed toward those who love him and are honest. How do you think that is expressed to us today?

DAILY ACTION ITEM:

- Find a picture of the ocean or a mountain on your phone or computer and leave it as your screen's picture to remind you of God's hugeness.

- Has God put something huge on your heart to do as you seek justice? If so, start praying about it.

PRAY:

Before you move on to what's next in your day, pray for the huge thing God has put on your heart or for a friend who needs to receive the love of God.

THOUGHTS:

This space is for any notes or thoughts you would like to write down.

DAY 19

Have you ever been treated unfairly? Of course you have. Maybe someone sent out a text about you that was not true or you got blamed for something in class that wasn't your fault. But for Lien, a teenage girl in Cambodia, being treated unfairly went to a whole different level. Both she and her sister accepted jobs at a coffee shop in a nearby town. But it wasn't a coffee shop—it was a brothel. They had been trafficked, and for the next three years they were trapped in a life that was anything but fair. If they refused to see the brothel's customers, they were beaten.

But then one day they were rescued by the Cambodian police and were placed in an aftercare home for trafficked victims. Slowly but surely Lien began to rebuild her life. She soon learned how to bake cupcakes and discovered she had a gift of making confectionary art. Now after graduating, Lien is one of the teachers at the same café where she learned her skills and is helping other girls recover from the abuse they were rescued from.

TODAY'S READING:

- Find today's verse, highlight it, and add today's date next to it in your own Bible.

- Read the verse several times, thinking about each word and asking God to help you understand what it means.

PSALM 103:6

The Lord gives righteousness and justice to all who are treated unfairly.

QUESTIONS TO THINK ABOUT:

- What types of people seem to be treated unfairly the most in our world? in your community? at your school?

- Can you think of a recent time when you or one of your friends was treated unfairly? What was unjust or not right about that situation?

- Write down some ways you think God gives righteousness and justice in situations of unfair treatment today.

- What are some ways God might use you to help those who are being treated unfairly at your school, in your community, or in our world?

DAILY ACTION ITEM:

- Make or buy some cupcakes and then give them to your friends at school this week as a way to share Lien's story.

PRAY:

Before you move on to what's next in your day, pause a few moments and pray for young people like Lien who are trapped in brothels and being treated unfairly. Ask God to quickly give righteousness and justice to them.

78

THOUGHTS:

This space is for any notes or thoughts you would like to write down.

To be the best in most sports—at any level of competition—requires ability, quickness, agility, and strength. And in some sports, the stronger you are, the better advantage you have over your opponent. I was recently at the gym with my nephew Tad, a wrestler in high school, and watched with amazement as he lifted a 245-pound set of free weights!

I also recently read about a high school football team in Ohio that used weightlifting to do more than simply get stronger for their team. They had an event called "Raising the Bar" designed to raise awareness and funds to fight human trafficking. Players decided to raise money based on how much weight they were able to lift as a team, and people sponsored them per pound lifted. These football players realized that using their strong arms could do more than just make them better players. The $5,000 they raised made it possible for people without the strength to defend themselves to have someone who's strong rescue them.

TODAY'S READING:

- Find today's passage, highlight it, and add today's date next to it in your own Bible.

- Read the passage several times, thinking about each word and asking God to help you understand what it means.

ISAIAH 59:15-16

Yes, truth is gone, and anyone who renounces evil is attacked. The Lord looked and was displeased to find there was no justice. He was amazed to see that no one intervened to help the oppressed. So he himself stepped in to save them with his strong arm, and his justice sustained him.

QUESTIONS TO THINK ABOUT:

- Why do people sometimes not intervene when corruption or injustice is happening around them?

- Think of a time when you or someone else stood up against something that was wrong but faced attacks or ridicule for what you or they said. How did that make you feel?

- What might help you stand up in the future against things that are wrong?

- What do you think of when you read about God stepping in with his strong arms?

- What might be some specific ways for you to intervene for the oppressed?

DAILY ACTION ITEM:

- Write the phrase "Seek Justice: Ask Me How" on a 3x5 card and tape it to the back of your cell phone. When asked, share about the slaves still trapped in today's world.

PRAY:

Before you move on to what's next in your day, pause a few moments and pray for the strength to stand up when you see or hear about something wrong happening at your school or in your community.

THOUGHTS:

This space is for any notes or thoughts you would like to write down.

DATE:

_____

As the owner of a rice mill, Kandasamy had lured his workers with one-time loans, assuring them they could work off the small loan in his factory. In reality, the loan was a trap and the people became his slaves. Kandasamy bragged openly about his profitable strategy, laughing as he explained: "The debt keeps accumulating....That is how I've run the business for 25 years now."

But then one day, IJM and the local authorities did a rescue operation at his rice mill and rescued 34 men, women, teenagers, and children. As the families learned to readjust to their new lives in a free society, IJM lawyers prepared a case against Kandasamy. Shockingly, when his trial concluded, he was sentenced to pay a mere 500 rupees— less than $10 in the U.S. The meaningless conviction emboldened Kandasamy to simply restock his rice mill with new slaves.

IJM began a second covert investigation. Again, armed with proof, IJM and the local authorities rescued over a dozen more slaves. A second trial began for Kandasamy, and this time he was convicted for his crimes and sentenced to five years in prison. He is no longer boasting about his slavery operations.

- Find today's passage, highlight it, and add today's date next to it in your own Bible.

- Read the passage several times, thinking about each word and asking God to help you understand what it means.

JEREMIAH 9:23-24

This is what the Lord says: "Don't let the wise boast in their wisdom, or the powerful boast in their power, or the rich boast in their riches. But those who wish to boast should boast in this alone: that they truly know me and understand that I am the Lord who demonstrates unfailing love and who brings justice and righteousness to the earth, and that I delight in these things. I, the Lord, have spoken!"

QUESTIONS TO THINK ABOUT:

- Circle the things in this passage that we should not boast about.

- Underline the things we should boast about.

- What might be the difference between good boasting and bad boasting?

- It is quite easy to boast of God's unfailing love, but how might you boast about God as he brings about justice?

DAILY ACTION ITEM:

- Share the story of Kandasamy with a friend or your family today—or check out IJM.org to find the latest stories that have happened in recent days and weeks.

PRAY:

Before you move on to what's next in your day, pause a few moments and pray for the slaves still trapped in rice mills like the one Kandasamy used to run. Pray for the hearts of slave owners like Kandasamy—that they would stop what they are doing.

THOUGHTS:

This space is for any notes or thoughts you would like to write down.

DATE:

_____

Do you remember being a child and participating in a school play or church choir performance, or maybe playing youth baseball or soccer? What was the first thing you did when you got on the stage, stepped into the batter's box, or ran across the field for the ball? You looked into the crowd to find your parents' faces and maybe even gave a little wave to them—even though they may have embarrassed you as they strived to get your attention.

Well, it doesn't change much as you get older. During each of the half marathons I have run, I'm always desperately looking for the friends and family who have come to cheer me on—especially at the finish line where I can give them a little wave or thumbs up, even though I'm exhausted. Have you ever thought what God looks like and wondered if he might be in the stands watching you?

TODAY'S READING:

- Find today's verses, highlight them, and add today's date next to them in your own Bible.

- Read the verses several times, thinking about each word and asking God to help you understand what these Scriptures mean.

PSALM 11:3-4, 7

"The foundations of law and order have collapsed. What can the righteous do?" But the Lord is in his holy Temple; the Lord still rules from heaven. He watches everyone closely, examining every person on earth....For the righteous Lord loves justice. The virtuous will see his face.

QUESTIONS TO THINK ABOUT:

- With all the huge injustices in the world today, it can seem hopeless at times. How might these verses bring encouragement to you and to others?

- What goes through your mind when you play a sport, perform a music piece, draw a picture, give a speech, or participate in any other event with family or friends watching you?

- What acts of justice might God be smiling at in your life as he watches you?

- Now make a mental picture of what it looks like to have God smiling at you and cheering you on from heaven—or draw an actual picture that somehow captures that scene or your feelings about it.

DAILY ACTION ITEM:

- What person in your life needs you in the stands cheering for them this week? Make a point to go to their game, concert, or event and be the one that they see smiling at them.

PRAY:

Before you move on to what's next in your day, pause a few moments and pray that you would be able to bring a smile to God today.

THOUGHTS:

This space is for any notes or thoughts you would like to write down.

Can you imagine wearing the same clothes for an entire month? I realize that for some guys, this wouldn't be a big deal. But seriously, ladies, would you sacrifice your whole wardrobe for an entire month for a cause? Well, that's what girls all across the country have been doing with a challenge called "One Dress, One Month, One Cause." The idea is to simply draw attention to human trafficking victims who only have one dress or shirt to wear, by just wearing one single dress for a whole month. Guys have been getting into this, too, by wearing the same shirt for an entire month.

Of course, participants don't have to wear the same dress or shirt to work out or sleep in, but for everything else, it's only one item. Many of the students who have done this also eliminate buying any type of clothing for the month and donate the money they might normally spend. One student, Lisa, went as far as creating a donation website and a daily Facebook® picture posting of how she accessorized her black dress each day—and she raised over $1,370. As you read today's Scripture, think about how this type of sacrifice might fit.

TODAY'S READING:

- Find today's passage, highlight it, and add today's date next to it in your own Bible.

- Read the passage several times, thinking about each word and asking God to help you understand what it means.

PROVERBS 21:2-3

People may be right in their own eyes, but the Lord examines their heart. The Lord is more pleased when we do what is right and just than when we offer him sacrifices.

QUESTIONS TO THINK ABOUT:

- How might doing what is right in your own eyes be different from what God sees in a person's heart?

- The idea that God examines your heart—do you find that encouraging or intimidating? Why?

- What happens in a community if everyone does what they think is right and there is no standard for everyone to follow?

- It's important to note that sacrifices (giving up something) are an important part of our faith. But why is God more pleased with justice and doing good deeds than with sacrifices?

DAILY ACTION ITEM:

- Think of something you could give up or sacrifice this week—and then donate what it costs to an effort or organization that promotes goodness or justice. Would you sacrifice your daily latte? movies? smoothie? music downloads? And where would you donate the money?

PRAY:

Before you move on to what's next in your day, pause a few moments and pray that God would reveal specific ways you can do what is good and just.

THOUGHTS:

This space is for any notes or thoughts you would like to write down.

Laughter and the crash of bowling pins tumbling down fill the air. A popular song begins to play, and dozens of girls shout and sing along. It could be an afternoon of fun anywhere in the world, but for the nearly 150 girls gathered in Kolkata, India, this afternoon is a standout event. The girls—many of them teenagers and some of them young mothers—have been rescued from their oppressors. They are sex trafficking survivors.

Every summer, IJM Kolkata hosts a day full of "summer camp" activities for trafficking survivors who live at the different aftercare homes in the city. "Hosting events like these is just one way to show the girls that we love them," says Anju Sherpa, an IJM caseworker who provides therapy and a stable relationship to many of the girls rescued in IJM-assisted operations. For Anju, these relationships often begin on the very night a girl is rescued from the brothel where she has been exploited. It takes time and patience and skill to bring healing and build trust. This day is important because it is simply a day to enjoy being a teenage girl who can dance and laugh with her friends. See how this story fits today's verses.

- Find today's verses, highlight them, and add today's date next to them in your own Bible.

- Read the verses several times, thinking about each word and asking God to help you understand what these Scriptures mean.

JEREMIAH 22:3, 16

" 'This is what the Lord says: Be fair-minded and just. Do what is right! Help those who have been robbed; rescue them from their oppressors. Quit your evil deeds! Do not mistreat foreigners, orphans, and widows.'...He gave justice and help to the poor and needy, and everything went well for him. Isn't that what it means to know me?" says the Lord.

QUESTIONS TO THINK ABOUT:

- Being fair-minded implies using your mind. How might using your mind cause you to be fair and just?

- What are some ways that people might be mistreated in your school or community?

- How can doing justice and helping the poor draw you closer to God?

- Who in your school or community needs your help? What are specific ways you can help them?

DAILY ACTION ITEM:

- Contact your community center, church, or local elementary school to find an upcoming fun children's type of event where you can volunteer your time to help.

PRAY:

Before you move on to what's next in your day, pause a few moments and pray for the girls who need to experience a fun day like the girls in Kolkata have.

THOUGHTS:

This space is for any notes or thoughts you would like to write down.

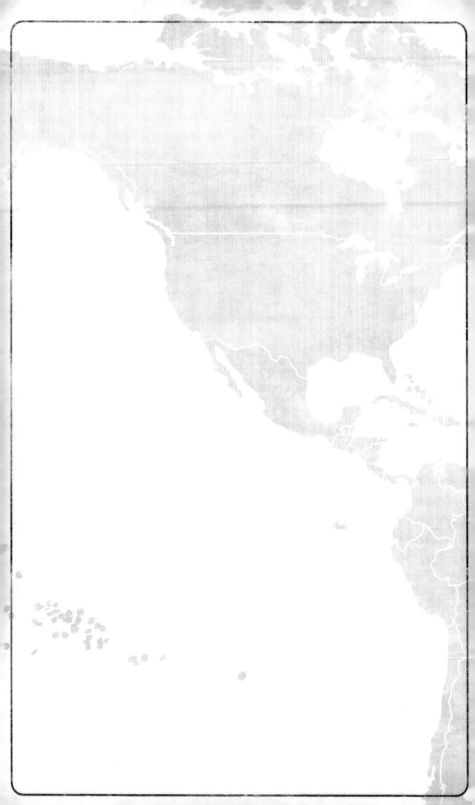

DAY 25

DATE:
_____

Growing up, I was the guy who read all the instructions in a game before we started or for a bike that needed to be put together, and I even read the manual when setting up the stereo system in my room as a teenager. That carried over into knowing all the rules in sports, at home, at school, at church, and in the Bible. I actually took pride in the fact that I not only knew all the rules, but I also followed them—and took pride in the fact that I was "better" than everyone else.

Here's the problem: At times I created my own interpretation of the rules and even made a few rules of my own. Sometimes I missed out on the joy of a game or became stressed out by doing what was "right" because I was so focused on rules. Jesus warns us about this in today's Scripture.

TODAY'S READING:

- Find today's verse, highlight it, and add today's date next to it in your own Bible.

- Read the verse several times, thinking about each word and asking God to help you understand what it means.

MATTHEW 23:23

"What sorrow awaits you teachers of religious law and you Pharisees. Hypocrites! For you are careful to tithe even the tiniest income from your herb gardens, but you ignore the more important aspects of the law—justice, mercy, and faith. You should tithe, yes, but do not neglect the more important things."

QUESTIONS TO THINK ABOUT:

- If you read all of Matthew 23, you'll see Jesus teaching about what it means to be a hypocrite—a person who says one thing but does another. Why do you think Jesus is so harsh toward the religious leaders in this verse?

- Why is it sometimes easy to ignore the important things Jesus mentions: justice, mercy, and faith?

- Why do you think justice was such an important issue to Jesus?

- Is there an area of your life where you might be a bit of a hypocrite and need to change? If so, what changes can you make, and what friends or trusted adults can help you in this area?

DAILY ACTION ITEM:

- On a 3x5 card or blank piece of paper write the word *Hypocrite* and then draw a red circle with a line through it over the word. Now post it on your bedroom door or bathroom mirror as a reminder for the rest of the month.

PRAY:

Before you move on to what's next in your day, pause a few moments and pray for the area in your life where you might be hypocritical and ignoring an issue of justice, mercy, or faith.

THOUGHTS:

This space is for any notes or thoughts you would like to write down.

DAY 26

DATE: _____

I remember walking to a professional baseball game in downtown Seattle with my family, when my son Marshall, who was 10 years old at the time, tugged on my arm and asked me for some money. I figured he wanted to buy a hot dog or peanuts, so I gave him $5. But to my surprise, as we were walking past a homeless person sitting on the sidewalk, Marshall stopped to ask this man if he was hungry—and simply gave the man his $5. While most people walked around this man, and I barely noticed him myself, Marshall had seen his need and gave what he had. In today's Scripture, Jesus answers the question, "Who is my neighbor?"

TODAY'S READING:

- Find today's passage, highlight it, and add today's date next to it in your own Bible.

- Read the passage several times, thinking about each word and asking God to help you understand what it means.

LUKE 10:30-37

"A Jewish man was traveling from Jerusalem down to Jericho, and he was attacked by bandits. They stripped him of his clothes, beat him up, and left him half dead beside the road. By chance a priest came along. But when he saw the man lying there, he crossed to the other side of the road and passed him by. A Temple assistant walked over and looked at him lying there, but he also passed by on the other side. Then a despised Samaritan came along, and when he saw the man, he felt compassion for him. Going over to him, the Samaritan soothed his wounds with olive oil and wine and bandaged them. Then he put the man on his own donkey and took him to an inn, where he took care of him. The next day he handed the innkeeper two silver coins, telling him, 'Take care of this man. If his bill runs higher than this, I'll pay you the next time I'm here.' Now which of these three would you say was a neighbor to the man who was attacked by bandits?" Jesus asked.

QUESTIONS TO THINK ABOUT:

- How would you answer Jesus' question at the end of this passage?

- Who might the different characters in this parable represent in our world today?

1. Temple Priest:

   _____

2. Temple Assistant:

   _____

3. Samaritan:

   _____

- What can keep you from helping people you see or know who have needs?

- What might have helped the Jewish man from being attacked in the first place?

DAILY ACTION ITEM:

- Dig into your pocket or purse and give some of your money to someone in need you see today, or to an organization that helps those in need.

PRAY:

Before you move on to what's next in your day, pause a few moments and pray for those in your school or community who need food, shelter, or medicine.

THOUGHTS:

This space is for any notes or thoughts you would like to write down.

Soccer fans have a reputation around the world as being the loudest, craziest, and most enthusiastic fans among all the sports. All you have to do is watch a European soccer game on TV to understand what I mean. I attended a professional soccer game last year, and a whole section of the stadium stood and shouted the entire game. Never sitting down, never stopping the cheering, jeering, and chanting the entire game! For a casual soccer fan, it was hard to see what they were so excited about.

But that all changed when I heard about some soccer-crazy students and teachers at Clover Hill High School in Virginia. They hosted a soccer game and asked the 400 people who attended to do something crazy as well. They asked everyone to enthusiastically donate money at the game to help rescue those who are oppressed and held as prisoners in modern-day slavery. Together they raised $1,700! Now, that is something we all can cheer about.

TODAY'S READING:

- Find today's verses, highlight them, and add today's date next to them in your own Bible.

- Read the verses several times, thinking about each word and asking God to help you understand what these Scriptures mean.

PSALM 146:1-2, 7

Praise the Lord! Let all that I am praise the Lord. I will praise the Lord as long as I live. I will sing praises to my God with my dying breath....He gives justice to the oppressed and food to the hungry. The Lord frees the prisoners.

QUESTIONS TO THINK ABOUT:

- What sports or events make you want to stand up and cheer, shout, and applaud?

- Verse 1 sounds like some excited soccer fans, doesn't it? Circle the three items in verse 7 that they are excited about.

- What are some of the ways that God actually does verse 7 today? Write out some of the ways you have heard organizations or people living out these actions of justice.

- What type of prisoner do you think the Lord frees? Why?

DAILY ACTION ITEM:

- On a piece of cardboard, write the phrase "I cheer for Justice" and then take pictures of friends holding the sign at school. Then post photos on social media using the hashtag #Icheerforjustice and see how many pictures you can collect.

- Looking for something big to do? Talk with your school about raising funds or collecting food at an upcoming sporting event. Give people something to really cheer about.

PRAY:

Before you move on to what's next in your day, pause a few moments and pray for ways that you can do more than just cheer at a game or concert.

THOUGHTS:

This space is for any notes or thoughts you would like to write down.

Some of my memories as a child are the times we did things as a family: road trips to Disneyland, camping in the woods, swimming and water-skiing on Lake Sammamish. But for Arjun, a young boy from Bangalore, India, all his family memories are from inside a brick kiln, where his father and mother were tricked into taking a loan designed to force them to be slaves. That all changed when IJM worked with local police to free his family along with 15 others.

But the road since rescue has not been easy. Arjun's father was killed in a tragic train accident—just after his mother had given birth to a third child. As a widow and single parent, she now has to care for her family on her own. Over the years, IJM has supported families like Arjun's as they rebuild lives of freedom—this support has allowed Arjun and his brothers to stay in school. Arjun is now able to create memories like many boys in India, playing soccer and going to school and being with his friends. And this has all reminded me that the greatest legacy and best memories my parents passed along to me involved serving others in need in our community.

- Find today's verses, highlight them, and add today's date next to them in your own Bible.

- Read the verses several times, thinking about each word and asking God to help you understand what these Scriptures mean.

JAMES 1:26-27

If you claim to be religious but don't control your tongue, you are fooling yourself, and your religion is worthless. Pure and genuine religion in the sight of God the Father means caring for orphans and widows in their distress and refusing to let the world corrupt you.

ISAIAH 1:17

"Learn to do good. Seek justice. Help the oppressed. Defend the cause of orphans. Fight for the rights of widows."

QUESTIONS TO THINK ABOUT:

- Why do you think James calls some "religion" worthless? What does worthless religion look like?

- Why is caring for orphans and widows so important to God?

- How do you see these passages—one from the New Testament and one from the Old Testament—complementing each other today? List out the ways that "pure and genuine religion" happens.

- How might the "world corrupt you" as you strive to live out your faith?

DAILY ACTION ITEM:

- Can you think of a widow or single parent in your neighborhood? Could you volunteer some time to help them this week with yard work, housework, babysitting, or some other specific need?

PRAY:

Before you move on to what's next in your day, pause a few moments and pray for the widows and orphans who still need someone to help them.

THOUGHTS:

This space is for any notes or thoughts you would like to write down.

What brings you joy—the feeling of great pleasure and happiness? For most people, it's when they use their gifts, skills, and passions together to accomplish something. For some it's making the shot in basketball, or playing the right notes when performing a song, or getting a new high score on a favorite video game, or helping a friend with their math homework.

For the students at the tae kwon do school and Evangelical Covenant youth group in Nelson, Canada, joy came by breaking boards with their bare hands at the "Break-a-Thon." The tae kwon do demonstration and board-breaking event was held at a local mall as part of "Champions of Freedom and Justice." I saw a video of the finale as they broke 27 boards representing the 27 million slaves still held captive in our world today. With those loud shouts, arms and legs flying, and boards breaking all over the place, I not only experienced joy in watching it, but also saw joy in the faces of the students as they used their gifts to help bring rescue to others.

TODAY'S READING:

- Find today's verses, highlight them, and add today's date next to them in your own Bible.

- Read the verses several times, thinking about each word and asking God to help you understand what these Scriptures mean.

PSALM 41:1

Oh, the joys of those who are kind to the poor!

PSALM 106:3

There is joy for those who deal justly with others and always do what is right.

PROVERBS 21:15

Justice is a joy to the godly, but it terrifies evildoers.

QUESTIONS TO THINK ABOUT:

- What brings you joy? List out two or three specific things.

- Why do you think people who help the poor experience deep joy?

- Can you think of some ways that people doing justice could experience joy?

- Why does justice terrify the evildoers?

DAILY ACTION ITEM:

- Select one of the ways you experience joy. How you can share that joy with someone who needs to experience your kindness?

- What might be a specific way you could use your gifts, talents, or skills to raise awareness for justice?

PRAY:

Before you move on to what's next in your day, pause a few moments and pray that those who work to bring justice for the poor would experience joy today.

THOUGHTS:

This space is for any notes or thoughts you would like to write down.

IJM lawyer Lisa went to a courthouse in Manila, the capital of the Philippines, where she'd been many times before. She was hoping that a case that she'd been working on for a long time would be coming to an end that afternoon. The case was against a trafficker who had abused and enslaved two girls. Lisa had been working her hardest to ensure that the trafficker would face just consequences under the law for this crime. But after years of experience, Lisa knows that just when a case seems like it should finally end, there are often delays. So Lisa showed up at the courthouse alone, fully expecting to simply be given a new date to come back on. Paint buckets were scattered everywhere, and the court was clearly under serious renovation.

But instead of a new date, Lisa was asked to go to a new courtroom in the building. The judge said the ruling would be delivered that very day. Lisa said she sat there praying, silently asking to hear words of justice and truth in that room. The judge read out the court's decision: The trafficker was found guilty of trafficking two girls and faced prison. It had been five years of court battles since the girls were rescued. Their past is very much in the past, and their future looks big, as these girls have just finished high school. And the girls' trafficker will not be terrifying anyone, anymore!

TODAY'S READING:

- Find today's passage, highlight it, and add today's date next to it in your own Bible.

- Read the passage several times, thinking about each word and asking God to help you understand what it means.

PSALM 10:17-18

Lord, you know the hopes of the helpless. Surely you will hear their cries and comfort them. You will bring justice to the orphans and the oppressed, so mere people can no longer terrify them.

QUESTIONS TO THINK ABOUT:

- Circle the words that explain what the Lord knows, what the Lord hears, and what the Lord does in these verses.

- What might be a definition of someone who is "helpless"?

- Do you at times feel helpless and wonder if God hears your cries? He does. What might be some hopes you feel helpless about?

- When have you experienced God's comfort?

DAILY ACTION ITEM:

- Do you know of anyone who feels helpless and needs to experience God's comfort? Is there a way you could be the one God uses to comfort them?

Give that person a call, or send an encouraging note, text, or email today.

PRAY:

Before you move on to what's next in your day, pause a few moments and pray for those are waiting for justice and comfort to happen for them.

THOUGHTS:

This space is for any notes or thoughts you would like to write down.

Well, you have made it to the end! Congratulations! These 31 devotions may have taken you a month or two or three to complete, but you did it. If you've been doing the action steps every day, I bet you've had a lot of conversations with people in your life—and you may have found yourself outside of your comfort zone a few times. When I finished running my first half marathon, I couldn't believe I'd completed it and proudly wore the medal I received at the finish line. I wish I had a medal to give you, but I hope your understanding of God's heart and passion for justice has caused your own heart to be more in line with his—and that's enough of a medal.

The stories you read of people who have been set free and those who have helped to set them free don't end today, though. That's because you are now part of the story of justice and freedom for others, too. God gave you gifts, skills, and talents to help others. If slavery is going to be abolished in your lifetime, then it will take you being part of the team to make it happen.

TODAY'S READING:

- Find today's verses, highlight them, and add today's date next to them in your own Bible.

- Read the verses several times, thinking about each word and asking God to help you understand what the Scriptures mean.

125

GALATIANS 5:1, 13-14

So Christ has truly set us free. Now make sure that you stay free, and don't get tied up again in slavery to the law....For you have been called to live in freedom, my brothers and sisters. But don't use your freedom to satisfy your sinful nature. Instead, use your freedom to serve one another in love. For the whole law can be summed up in this one command: "Love your neighbor as yourself."

QUESTIONS TO THINK ABOUT:

- In these verses, how do slavery and freedom illustrate what Christ has done for us?

- How might we be "free" but still enslaved to sin?

- What sometimes makes it hard to serve others in love?

- What specific person has God called you to love and serve? How can you put that love into action this week?

DAILY ACTION ITEM:

- Review the reading plan you made on Day Zero and revise as needed for the next 31 days. Selecting a new topic or book of the Bible you are interested in, and dive in!

PRAY:

Before you move on to what's next in your day, pause a few moments and pray for the people who have been set free since you started this devotional.

THOUGHTS:

This space is for any notes or thoughts you would like to write down.

YOUR NEXT 31 DAYS

1. **Don't stop reading your Bible.** Take the time to renew a plan like you created on Day Zero.

   - Ask a friend or youth pastor for some ideas on what might be good for you.

2. **You can find other great student devotional books at simplyyouthministry.com**

3. **Looking for more ways to get involved with the International Justice Mission?**

   - Host a "24-Hour Justice Experience" with your youth group. Go to IJM.org/24JE to receive the free materials.

   - Invite an IJM speaker to your church, youth group, school assembly, or school chapel. Go to IJM.org/get-involved

   - Start a Justice Club on your school with the Justice Club toolkit. Go to IJM.org/get-involved/youth

   - Sign up for IJMhq on Instagram® to receive weekly pictures and updates

   - Download the IJM app on your phone